Norman Nicholson
by Chris Barnfather

Between Comets

Between Comets

for Norman Nicholson at 70

Edited by

WILLIAM SCAMMELL

TAXVS

1984

ISBN 1 85019 011 9 (paperback, first printing 700 copies)
ISBN 1 85019 012 7 (boards, edition limited to 50 copies)
ISBN 1 85019 013 5 (boards, single presentation copy)

Published by
TAXVS PRESS,
30 Logan Street,
Langley Park,
Durham DH7 9YN.

Set in 11 on 12pt Baskerville and printed by
CWS Printing Works, Gateshead, Tyne & Wear.

Cloth editions bound by Woolnough Fine Bindings,
Irthlingborough, Northamptonshire.

CONTRIBUTORS

Introduction

Norman Nicholson is 70 this year. For fifty years he has pursued his vocation, which is a lonely and difficult one, with the greatest distinction. We offer him this tribute in honour of his life and work.

My thanks to all the contributors, who responded so warmly to the invitation to join in this celebratory volume. Two of them summed up the esteem in which both the man and the poet are held. 'He is exemplary in the way he has gone about his work for a long time, quietly and without fuss,' said John Montague; and Seamus Heaney wrote 'His name is surrounded with fondness in my head.'

I should also like to thank Michael Farley, who designed this book and saw it expertly through the press; Matt Simpson for his encouragement and support; Faber & Faber for permission to quote from Norman's works; and Fraser Steel, who suggested the title.

*   *   *   *

For Norman Nicholson 'history' necessarily comes 'Squinting over the rim of the fell' ('From a Boat at Coniston'), since the fells stop just short of his back yard. What the yard, the fells and the lakes speak of – 'My sight lengthens its focus' – is both local and universal:

> I wait for the wind to drop, against hope
> Hoping, and against the weather, yet to see
> The water empty, the water full of itself,
> Free of the sky and the cloud and free of me.

'Free of' is acutely ambivalent here (not least in its twin subjects, 'I' and 'the water'), meaning both 'rid of' and 'made free of', licensed to know himself only by knowing his not-self, which is nature and natural death. From the very beginning of the poem the lake is 'my own face', the mounting paradoxes beautifully prefigured in the picture of the water 'Black with sunset'. The poem explores a whole nexus of inner-outer relationships, in a manner reminiscent of Wordsworth yet thoroughly contemporary, and dignifies a stock image ('the element of mirrors') with delightful new life won from the poet's own humanity, which owes as much to cultural as to literal geology. Once he had found a way round or through Wordsworth, the great genius of the place ('To the River Duddon' is both homage and pious riddance), he gave back a voice to the landscape that had gravelled his own to a whisper.

This is simply to say, in other words, that the poems are as much a product of Nicholson's reading and sensibility as they are of his birthplace. For all the neat parallelism between his craggy verbal and natural resources – 'neb', 'cruck', 'sneck', 'slag' etc. – it is a hard-won art that raises his oeuvre above local patriotism; what he himself has called, in another context, 'My virtuosity of print' ('Have You Been to London?'). By a freak of publishing history his first public outing was made in the company of Keith Douglas (see the bibliography on p65), and the young man who hadn't been either to London or to war took his place alongside the most brilliant English poet of the mid-century. Yet neither his habitual modesty ('Damn all but hem/And haw...') nor the apparently restricted scope of his endeavour have hindered his recognition as a poet of the first rank, one who has lived long enough to see time's whirligig restore his kind of honesty to the forefront of poetic taste.

Another part of his inheritance has to do with gentleness and fortitude. Though never given to self-pity, his poems are open to a deal of tenderness and compassion, both towards himself and others. It is no accident, I think, that he has written so well about Cowper, the 'stricken deer' of early Romanticism. His fine poem 'Cowper's Tame Hare' says as much about the man as any biography; and handles its underlying theme of madness and despair with a tact all but lost on some of the confessional poets of recent times. 'She came to him in dreams – her ears/Diddering like antennae, and her eyes/Wide as dark flowers where the dew/Holds and dissolves a purple hoard of shadow.' Other poets might have written the first two lines, striking though they are; but the quiet and beautiful exactitude of their continuation is a triumph peculiar to Nicholson, in which feeling and technique are fused together in the service of a visionary miniaturism peculiarly appropriate to his subject.

The same ability to alter his focus informs the wry humour of poems such as 'Five Minutes', with its wonderful last line, 'Young Him', and the honest urbanities of 'Nicholson, Suddenly'. Who else would describe the end of an eclipse in such a homely image as lights up 'Great Day': 'Two minutes later/The twist of the globe turned up the dimmer/And day began again to try to begin'? The move from one world to another – the great globe itself wittily dissolving into the tiny globe of the gas bracket – is characteristic of a poet who moves easily between such gigantic disparities as 'five minutes' and 'the end of time', or from the 'piltdown grunt' to the vivid colloquialisms of Cumbrian speech.

Taking a hint, perhaps, from the 'holy smother' of 'The Seventeenth of the Name', the image of a gas bracket turns up again in the title poem of Norman's most recent collection *Sea to the West*:

> When the sea's to the West
> The evenings are one dazzle –
> You can find no sign of water.
> Sun upflows the horizon;
> Waves of shine
> Heave, crest, fracture,
> Explode on the shore;
> The wide day burns
> In the incandescent mantle of the air.

For ponderable reasons, the globe has now become a 'mantle', charged with Christian overtones. 'Let my eyes at the last be blinded/Not by the dark/But by dazzle,' he says at the end of the poem, and we note both the perkiness of the final word (quite different from Wordsworth's 'Clouds that gather round the setting sun'?) and the rhythmical modesty of its feminine ending, shorn of any definite or indefinite article.

Milan Kundera said recently that a writer's capital is contained in the first 20 or 30 years of his life, and this is borne out by Norman's poetry, which returns again and again to the infinitely precious particulars of Millom and home. Thanks to him we know it as well as we know Eastwood, Haworth and Bockhampton. Though he 'couldn't say *Boo* to a goose' and was packed off to 'dry dock' for early repair, he has gone on a splendid voyage, and spoken for us all.

WILLIAM SCAMMELL
Cockermouth, 1984.

11

Poem for the Seventieth Birthday of
Norman Nicholson

HOW

To bring greetings to a poet one has never met,
So far, over Pentland Firth and Grampians
And on and over the surging Borders
To the place where "a wall walks slowly"?
The first thing to do
Is, put on your coat of words,
And harp at a fishing village
For a crab or a herring,
And at a pub door
For a pint and a pie and a seat at the fire.
Maybe for some farmer in the Lothians
You will sing for your supper
And he'll give you a bed in his barn.
(And all this journey is made
In the time it takes to chant a ballad,
For poet lives next door to poet
In the good Village of Poetry,
Though their houses are scattered
From Iceland to Ecuador, and further.)
So I come at last to an honoured door,
Poem in pocket
And greetings and praise in my mouth
While inside
The seventy candles burn bright.

GEORGE MACKAY BROWN

Under Mount Rundle

Here comes the little Cornishman, steering
West over the hard swamp and sedge, by winter
Birch and willow. 1841. He wears
Lamb's wool next the skin, a muster of shirts,
Lined trousers, leggings, pilot-coat, moccasins,
A sealskin cap screwed down against the weather.
He is the Reverend Robert Terrill Rundle
Aged 29: 'young, inexperienced,
Of no obvious fitness for his calling.'

His loves are missionising and the mountains.
Born, Mylor, parish of ilex, oak and water.
He flags a mile behind the sled; is disconcerted
At scrawls of blood on the snow from the beaten huskies;
At the delegation of Blackfoot – 'so blackly painted
In history' – that greets him with kisses, prayers, the left
Hand given 'because it is nearest the heart.' The snow
Scores its harsh testament on the plain; goes missing.
He reads. Walks into the broken jaw of the Rockies.

CHARLES CAUSLEY

To The Glass-Blowers

The problem is one of how to paint
An empty wineglass in full sunlight
On a windowsill so as to capture

Those complicities of glass and light
Which at times suggest the glass may be
A consummation of the spirit

Of the light, even while it flings
It off in prism; to capture
Not only the essence and the past

But also the potential; not simply
What things are, but the power of what
They might just possibly become:

The quest which, with their retorts and stills,
Their crucibles and limbecks, alchemists
From Paracelsus down to Jonson's Subtle

All set themselves, pitting opposite against
Elemental opposite in that secret war,
And so busily they failed to notice

How in Venice, craftsmen in overalls
Were putting earth – through sand and potash –
To a trial by fire, and their gaffer,

As they called him, once that red
Gob of the metal was twirling through his fingers,
Breathing into it of his own human spirit.

                                        NEIL CURRY

Fresh growth

Left to itself, the tea-rose 'Velia'
under the farthest corner of the wall
has quietly researched into its roots.
There was nobody to pay it much attention.

Old rigid stems with blood-inspiring thorns
die back, abandoned. Detailed fronds
arch out in every fresh direction
dizzy with spines, and insolently green.
They may, perhaps, be offshoots of the wall
which seems mature enough to flower now.

Gone is the toffee-sticky scent, the poster-paint
heads-up-while-on-parade display;
like a songbird in a mist net,
snagged here is the wild strain.
Open as innocence, pink as palms
these flowers, for all their visual fragility
and modesty of perfume, have displaced
the best that big investors could contrive.

They have stabbed to death a little apple tree;
best not to stand too close too long
to defiance growing stronger by the hour.
The failing wall will now renew itself.
The tranquil underground still
waits, then breaks out with its savage rose.

LYN DAWES

Bless the Bed that I Lie on

i.m. Marion Elliot, née Margaret Stewart Nedd,
1859 – Lochmore, 1955

The history of this blanket's partly known:
You made it – starting not from yarn but wool
Sheared perhaps from a known sheep in Glencoul,
And lichen, from the ultrabasic stone.

But is it older than your grandson? – made
Before your blindness, when you were a wife,
In the middle of your long pseudonymous life?
Or in my teens, when you were half a shade?

Is it your photograph I recall, or you,
In black against a white wall in the sun
Turning your wheel?

                  I'd like to think you spun
And dyed and wove my blanket in Glendhu,
Still in the drystone park like paradise
In summer

           – even that it kept you warm
That night beside your husband's mortal form,
Waiting together for the sun to rise.

ALISTAIR ELLIOT

For Norman Nicholson (70)

It's a very good thing all poets
don't write in exactly the same way –
imagine hundreds of clones of Craig Raine, Heaney,
Hughes!

There's room for all kinds of writing,
nothing, thank God, is laid down by law
(as, more or less, in some countries)! Different me's and
you's

can flourish: the townee, all tailored
in sophistication and waistcoated suits,
the isolated rustic who doesn't care for champagne,

some who go for wit, some for landscape,
traditional or experimental (some experiments fail) –
there are many different kinds, not just the pearl and the
plain.

Excellence in a kind is what we are after
(Shakespeare had it in most, if not all)
and your kind is yours, local and unique –

not boring, voulu, fake-homespun,
but very much the genuine thing,
coming in interesting shapes – for us all and not any man's
clique!

GAVIN EWART

For Norman Nicholson's Seventieth Birthday

It's three score year and ten
Sin' tha wert born   *since*
In th'ouse tha dwells in now –
Some record, Norm!

A envy thee, tha knows:
It mak's me sad
A left mi own town and folk
When nobbut a lad.   *only*

To me t'owd way of talk
Ull rarely come,   *will*
E'en now at times A feel
A'm far from whom.   *home*

'Appen because thou stuck
To Cumbria's scene
Thy words are reet wick still,   *very lively*
Sharp thy owd een.   *old eyes*

A think it were in that book
Of '43
Wi' Douglas and J. C. 'All,   *Keith Douglas and J. C. Hall*
A first read thee.

Like 'little nigger fists',
The blackberry
(Tha wrote then), compound like
A buzzer's e'e.   *bluebottle's eye*

Go on years more, owd lad,
To gie's a surprise   *give us*
With what *thy* compound e'e
Round th'ouse espies.

ROY FULLER

19

Rites of Passage

Comfortable words, framed
in darker times than ours,
are ruined archways,

rusted gates, lych gate
or kissing gate, beaten paths
to love or death

that dwindle out of use.
As our forefathers knew,
their ways are grass

– a by-way their sense of
comfortable, a castle stump
in the marches

that marks where a language
lost its fight. The formless
is given ground.

A name thumbed off the map
wears a way back to
the capital.

Death blues a nail, and
climbs the ring finger
to the heart.

We are raided by
the inarticulate. *Be sober,
be vigilant,*

the Apostle says – watchwords since
requisitioned by General Booth
and Captain Lynch

while *our adversary*...
as a roaring lion is
all but extinct.

The last enemy is
amnesia. The synapses
lapse in the mind,

the keystones fall to the grass.

ROGER GARFITT

(from a poem in progress)

A Paved Text

For Norman Nicholson

Dialect landlocked
in a maritime district,
stone walls in earshot
of rowlocks and the seawrack –

those Cumbrian phonetics
cracked like a plaited whip
until the slack, nostalgic
ambler in me trotted

on the paved margin
of my own black pool –
Dublin, black pool, *dubh linn*
in words beyond the Pale,

beyond Windscale, and Moyle
that sank in the North Channel.
Now nuclear poisons
re-anglicize a sea

that is yours and mine as well,
our saint-crossed, whitecapped, scouse-cursed
swan-road and path of exile
become a dump for waste.

Windscale: it was pristine,
imagined and self-cleansing
as the young, spray-blown Setanta
at his feats with a *caman* –

say bat, or better, hurley –
striking a silver ball,
skimming ahead on the waves
to intercept its fall.

Setanta, doomed name also,
not yet the *Hound* of *Ulster*,
Cuchulain, guardian, hero,
dangerous wave-beheader.

SEAMUS HEANEY

To Norman Nicholson, Rising Seventy One

As you avowedly have served your time
under the edged, striding shadow of Long Willie,
so we, soft-footed sidesmen
in the working nave of your plenty,
continually must check our données
– images, diction, ways of seeing –
against the definitive, northern tang.
So, should a line find us about the beck
and it's fizzling like ginger pop,
we can smirk but need to look further;
to the name on the bottle...
most times yours, of course.
And we'll have done it once more –
echoed, overheard, slipped
in the living scree of that voice –
and be at the bottom again,
rubbing ruefully, looking up.
But at least have stumbled on reality –
what's more, recognised it as such –
giving it Wigan, unearthed Normandy.

Normandy. Cartographers try to con us
it's over there, over 't' girt beck'.
They can ship their la-di-da somewhere else.
Because here's ·where it simmers,
the map behind the map. And starts at Millom:
that sea lion brandishing the thrilling rest
on the prodigious tip of its nose.
If you didn't invent it, you logged it between you
–you and that canny off-comer Wainwright –
he walking compasses, you words.

Whatever – it's done now, the work, the welding:
paraded solid on umpteen shelves.
As for your pet ambition, to see Halley's Comet –
here's hoping you'll notch up sight of it yet
and when it scalds your eye it sees you
–like Magritte's eagle in 'The Domain Of Arnheim' –
spliced into the very rock: what else but Black Combe –
indestructible, snowy sideburns and all.

GEOFFREY HOLLOWAY

A Tern
For Norman Nicholson

The breaker humps its green glass.
You see the sunrise through it, the wrack dark in it,
And over it — the bird of sickles
Swimming in the wind, with oiled spasm.

That is the tern. A blood-tipped harpoon
Hollow-ground in the roller-dazzle,
Honed in the wind-flash, polished
For her own expertise,

Now finished and in use.
The wings — remote-controlled
By the eyes
In her submarine swift shadow —

Feint and tilt in their steel.
Suddenly a powerful elastic
Connects her downward, through a thin shatter,
To a sand-eel. She hoists out, with a twinkling,

Through some other wave-window.
Her eye is a gimlet.
Deep in the churned grain of the roller
Her brain is a gimlet. She hangs

A blown tatter, a precarious word
Hovering in the mouth of ocean pronouncements.
Priestess of this place. She shudders
To the tips of her tail-tines —

Momentarily, her lit scrap is a shriek.

TED HUGHES

Markings

for Sarah

1

The markings almost disappear
With the shadowy sound you make
Launching the feather from your hand,
As though you would learn to whistle
By answering the curlew's cry.

2

I would remember tumblers
Above the water-meadow,
The shimmer of white feathers
In the flower-dwarfing wind,

Brood-patch and bird-brain,
The hummock of her body
That tries to make head or tail
Of movements inside the shell.

All that remains to show you
Is the deserted nest-bowl,
Blots and scribbles on an egg,
The dappled flight of lapwings.

3

One more pebble on the cairn
Might make it a vantage point
For the stonechat, a headstone
Should winter blow out his song,
His chestnut breast a tinderbox
Igniting the few syllables.

MICHAEL LONGLEY

Aldeburgh Moot Hall

'Horas non numero nisi serenas' — Inscription on the sundial

Words from a sundial: "The only
  hours I count are tranquil,
    the only days fine".
How few, though, the hours
  worth counting from that angle
    on which the sun must shine!

It seems a subtle hint
  that you, though centuries old,
    are in real terms a stripling,
having purged your calendar
  of weather or mood whose hold
    was harsh or crippling.

This worn brick and weathered
  timber give the lie
    to such a fantasy;
recall untranquil hours when
  the Hall seemed sure to die,
    a prize for the invading sea.

No true tranquillity
  can fill those who are blind
    to all untranquil times:
maybe its purest peace
  is what the Borough found
    when purged of Peter Grimes.

Yet I'm inclined to take
  the sundial's cure for cares:
    I cancel gravity –
and find, now, that I've clocked up
  a mere seven years
    when I'm approaching seventy!

EDWARD LOWBURY

By the Graveyard, Luskentyre

From behind the wall death sends out messages
That all mean the same, that are easy to understand.

But who can interpret the blue-green waves
That never stop talking, shouting, wheedling?

Messages everywhere. Scholars, I plead with you,
Where are your dictionaries of the wind, the grasses?

Four larks are singing in a showering sprinkle
Their bright testaments: in a foreign language.

And always the beach is oghamed and cuneiformed
By knot and dunlin and countrydancing sandpipers.

— There's Donnie's lugsail. He's off to the lobsters.
The mast tilts to the north, the boat sails west.

A dictionary of him? Can you imagine it? —
A volume thick as the height of the Clisham,

A volume big as the whole of Harris,
A volume beyond the wit of scholars.

NORMAN MACCAIG

Lindal Tunnel

Two long lifetimes ago, when they piled up this portal,
The view did the side-stroke, but the song is the same –
        Be there too soon, too soon.
Now, it's a gunbarrel seen round the driver's head.

Fish-glints of light all the way. The walls run and shine
By the jags of the stone, left in that way to save money.
        No need to be there too soon.
Only a minute or two, and the world of men's at the end.

The engineer's wit, when they cut through Crooklands,
Said leave room for two lines. Then twenty thousand trains
        clanged their rumbling tune.
A million lives scraped bits along these walls.

And miners jumped down, and then left the main line
To plod the red lanes, now silent and cemetery green.
        No need to be there too soon.
Then, the mines called and span, and the tramways sang.

Men went as the mines halted. The last whistle moaned.
Men sat dulled with their gear as the dark walls passed.
        Going to be there too soon.
They saw African gold at the end of a faraway line.

Some came back with the lung-dust. They saw the green
Of their lives as lads, as the tunnel welcomed them.
        We knew you'd be here too soon.
Back to a breathless chair to die in the peace of home.

        J. D. MARSHALL

Peninsula

Places where few come
mother earth sprouts
her natural defences;
jagged yellow gorse
poison ivy and oak,
tugging, tangled briars.

Beneath harsh brambles
a hoard of blackberries,
swarthy gouts of juice.
Under crimson skirts
of fuschia, bees hover
to cling for nectar.

Creaking crabs' claws
defend warm coves;
translucent parachutes
of stinging jellyfish
(flaccid heart valves,
pulsing, expanding).

Bladders of seawrack
lift to disclose a
skyblue bed of mussels:
spiky urchins crouch
in yellow rock pools.
Pursed oysters drowse.

To drift, lazily,
scarcely disturbing
the tidal rhythms,
kin to the waterstrider,
keeping company with
a shoal of fish.

Feathery pines, below
long folded mountains;
the light always shifting.
On a seaweeded rock
a solemnity of gulls,
chattering, staring.

The act of attention
as when swaying home
from the spring well
with a brimming bucket;
its trembling meniscus
water's hymen.

To stand stockstill
until a butterfly
alights on your arm,
steadying small sails;
scarlet spots upon
an ochre ground.

Dame nature's self
delighting richness;
in a clump of iris
a grasshopper shrills.
In the midge-thick twilight
a sea trout flails.

Abruptly in the bay
a school of dolphin
rehearsing their turns,
thrashing the water
with their flat tails;
exultant windmills!

JOHN MONTAGUE

Epithalamium for a Niece

'Who gives this woman to this man?'
The parson asks, and one man can,
According to the liturgy,
Rightly reply. And many more,
If saying 'I do' were the door
To show their daughters out, would say
It now and twenty times a day.
But with 'I do' or merely 'Me',
Failing the Prayer Book's nudge, who'd claim
Just cause or just justification
To dare the pride of giving? Let
Church and choir and congregation
Silent remain and the reply
Come from some other than the 'I'
That hesitates at 'Do'. The wind
Might say: 'I gave her breath'; the sky:
'I gave the light to see her by';
Soil and humus, stem and stone:
'We gave the calcium for the bone,
Carbohydrates, minerals, those
Hormones and genes and chromosomes
That chose her sex and shaped her nose'.
Water might lap and lip: 'From me
Venus was born, so why not she?'
But neither earth nor sky nor water
Speak sponsorship for this their daughter.
So in the eternity before
'I do' is done, and while the air
Waits on the Prayer Book's questionnaire,
Let silence ring its loud reply;
'She gives herself– what can a man ask more?'

NORMAN NICHOLSON

Stones lie...

Stones lie inert, of course.
They turn in profligate rain

So slightly.
You observe their smoothness, their edges

But do not see their moving.
They take their time —

Quartz time: flint time, time of bloodstone,
Time for landscapes to settle,

As though they were immobile,
As though their stones lay unmoved,

Aglow with rain, glowing
With the spendthrift rain...

You'd call them inscrutable — you haven't changed!
Unchanging, they gleam like stones,

Turn their absent eye
Not at all.

CHRISTOPHER PILLING

Going Home

This morning we escort Sharon,
who cannot talk.
Hugging her suitcase
she clumps to the back seat.
Her forearm is picked scabs,
knuckles misshapen.
When she left, the squawking
hurt our ears.
Nineteen, a bonny girl.
At her first period she screamed.
She strokes my hand, then her suitcase.
Her blunt moans speak pleasure.
The small hills make her ears pop –
that much I understand.
Her hands form flippers, penguin.
She swims to me. We laugh.
My shoulder aches from holding hands
across the seatback.

PATRICIA POGSON

Praising Colours

Suffolk houses imitate the sky's high flush,
Those madder shades of the sunstruck dusk,
And an earthy plenitude of tones
The county gives like wine.
These homes are bright compartments
In street-long exhibition lines,
Depictions of cloud colours I watch coming
And going, in late afternoons
When February days in England ache
And stretch their ruddled minutes
Longer before the dark.

Here I see vermilion paling
To a mallow pink, dun winter grey,
Sunny ochres, that brown-rheumed green
The Stour has, and the alluring tropic's
Persimmon-flaring paradox:
Terraced hues of earth and river
And cloudy sunset kept for good,
As if, knowing in the dark all colours
Will agree, men and women set their hearts
By day on living well inside their praise.

RODNEY PYBUS

Redmond's Hare

Tender as an osteopath,
I turned the stiff neck
to study the four long teeth
clenched like a mortise lock

and took in the dirty blur
of an eye out of focus,
the tiny windswept acres
of black and gold fur,

the penury of sodden paws.
The ears were glove fingers
squeezed through a wringer.
I jiggled a broken claw,

then felt the hard nipples
like a series of shocks,
simple but incredible,
and looked out the sex:

female, a little black-eye,
too tender to touch,
which only looked at me
and I was crushed

and had to look away.
So I got her undressed,
stiff as a child in a vest
and wild at the end of the day.

CRAIG RAINE

Placebo

The pine-tree knotted with resin,
At noon-day a flame.
The strange caverns in the headland.

The birds that sing inwardly, but sweetly.

Among the strange caverns in Langland
Is *Placebo*, the colloquial term
For the office of the dead,

And there are strange caverns
Elsewhere and everywhere.

Above the caverns
The thin tube of a wheatstraw bears the heavy ear
And above the caverns
The white butterfly flutters like a star
On the old stone wall
And in the butterfly is a cavern:
A-day-ago-it-was-not;
A dead thing
With claws crossed on chest,
It was mummified

And before that it was a slinking worm.

Now the new butterflies
Flutter like ironed hankies
On the ancient stone, or like stars
Waking in the old sky.

Passages, holes, prisons
And cataracts of water in every thing.
The pine-tree knotted with resin
At noon-day a planetarium
And myself
Walking the wall
Every day

In all weathers
Religiously
Among the glad flames
That please the dead
Even in the ashy frosts
When they hang everywhere and chime
All the stones gleaming deep as caverns
With the icy air as if polished by a blowflame.

PETER REDGROVE

Threescore and Ten

Praestet fides supplementum
Sensuum defectui.

In every generation
The young acquire an image of their elders
Tranquil, assured, with every day mapped out
From punctual meals to reading by the fire.
Threescore and ten is not like that at all
We find on getting there. Life is not tranquil,
But someone else has come into the room
And looks at us from time to time.
                                        To admit
He's there is one thing, but the trick is harder
To welcome and ignore him. For it seems
The old should live as though their days were endless,
Yet also, feeling the glance of death upon them
Think that all time is Now, waken the power
Which looks athwart our days to what's immortal,
The Third Eye, which sees where sense is dark.

ANNE RIDLER

Vocation

Is it poetry I'm after at these moments when
I must clothe your hands in mine or comfort your shoulders
–so bare and neglected sometimes when we wake –
or press your mouth to taste its uncurling flower?
Is that which seems so fleshly and truthful merely
a twisted track into words, a way to leave you
for your image? Art is tempting, a colourful
infidelity with the self, and doubly feigning
when what is re-possessed secretly by one
was made by two. And I wish I could pour a poetry-vodka
into twin glasses we'd gulp unanimously
("I poison myself for your health" the appropriate toast)
but only a poet would have acquired the taste
for such a strange distillation; you'd never warm
to heavy-petting dactyls, the squeak and creak
from locked, suburban stanzas. And so my fingers,
dancing alone, are less than content. They perceive
how they have clung to moral adolescence.
Their vocation now could be simply to talk to your skin,
to take you at kissing-time; later, to close your eyes
by stroking the lashes lightly over cheekbones
flushed with some high, bright, childish fever, and so
write the poem in the touch-shapes of darkness
and let it end there . . . . They are on the tip of trusting
this silent, greyish room, its astonishing view
fading from metaphor to the life with you.

CAROL RUMENS

40

Ten Miles for a Kiss

'One of the grand
spectacles of the universe'
is Reverend Francis Kilvert
taking his bearings among

'these mountain beauties':
Prissy Prosser, Hetty Gore,
Polly Greenway, Gypsy Lizzie,
Emmeline, Lucretia, Jenny Dew...

adjectives bubbling down
the reaches of his eye.
Hard by Capel-y-Ffin
where monkish men

are sweating in
their habits, digging
deep to build, a girl
sings at her washbowl

'up to the elbows
of her round
white lusty arms
in soapsuds.'

Cwm and dingle, moon
frost, dew, mesmeric
glut of light
upon Plynlimmon

and on fallers
bedded in lush grass
receive their blessing
from the midmost centre

of a curate's heart,
whose calling card's a cowslip
tendered to the warm
snout of a latch.

The 'pure fair sweet
grave face' of Annie Dyke
is not at home today;
'ten miles for a kiss'

he'll just have
to imagine...and
he will. The air is fat
as a baby's wrist,

unlike Cornwall, where
'the smell of fish is sometimes
so terrific as to stop
the church clock dead.'

Noses notwithstanding, nor
the 'concubinage' of Myra Rees
nor clergyman's daughters
out castrating lambs

('I forgave them')
nor May Eve witches
old and young ('the young
...are welcome')

nor a starving cat
that perches in the hovel
of old Pritchard's
guttering life

nor drunken fair days
nor the parish pauper
after a lifetime's labour
slashing his gizzard

to haul out the keck...
there's archery and croquet,
boating, picnics, racy
novels by Ouida

('how that woman hates
her sex'), beacon-haunted
Hay-on-Wye hugging
its golden pelt

where mayflies
stitch their cope
in the setting sun
and, after rain, the river

flashes off
like a frightened snake.

WILLIAM SCAMMELL

A Visit to Millom

for Norman Nicholson

It was a long way round from
Ulverston on the bus to Millom.
We passed the low sands and the gulls
and the first outcrop of the hills
until at 'the west of the west'
– his phrase – we reached a film set
of the 1930's, stage and props.
You could tread on a whole row of shops
and chapels. So many corners to lean against.
So much shoring up of the corrugated fence.
That must be the house
with its old shop window doused,
where you can sit at the back
and join in the front street crack.
Over the roofs, Black Combe,
and yonder the silent doom
of Windscale. All this has been set
down in words, from the Good Friday sonnet
of the first wartime anthology
to the dazzle of the Easter Sunday sea.

DAVID SCOTT

High Kingdom

Climbing the beanstalk of your mind, I reach
a star, the private country you inhabit,
where no adult proprieties encroach
upon the candleflame that is your spirit.

A myriad landscapes lie within your eyes.
Here Hamelin shadows caper to piping light;
castles rise and crumble with miraculous ease
but leave no hurt perceptions in the heart.

Wind sings its crazy swallows over lake
and shallow river, or thoughtfully carves
a symphony in stone: wind your broomstick,
you mark the intimations of the leaves.

And here the wild white horses of your will –
such fallible gods to hasten your footsteps –
leap, as my hand leaps, or this eager wall,
when you balance my world on finger tips.

No time no seasons urging, you salvage
every idle minute with your child-true
faculty for indiscriminate coinage;
importunate twig, absorb the whole tree.

Names have no meaning, eyes mean what they say
(later, perhaps, you'll learn to parry truth
with words). Each day an adventure, you see
parents as mountains moving by your faith.

HOWARD SERGEANT

A Man from the Shipyards

In the process of becoming a Quaker, Penn, still in the navy, asked whether, or not, or for how long, he should continue to wear his sword. 'Wear it,' Fox answered, 'for as long as thou canst.'

'In the destructive element immerse' *Lord Jim*, Conrad

Penn, from the shipyards, bears a sword. 'Natural
to a man of war.' 'What must I do with it?'
Fox answers, 'Wear it as long as thou canst.' Thou is
thou yet. Although that natural, aching
psyche in its wet plasm of snowy
righteousness requires, 'your life for my child's.'
That some women
are not made more compassionate than all men.

As if for arbitration, bearing a sword
Penn leads the beasts – a forest clearing, by leaves
melted to twilight, the sword
like a bird, rustling, biting
the leaves, to line its children's nest. And not
much different, she – the human animal –
pulls his senses to her breasts annulling
jealousy. Penn works, changing
each creature to a humane form, the sinewy mind
all-eyed, spotting like
a candle in snow. Penn and Fox

smudge with earth, lying between
creatures, digesting the consequences
of hunger. They speak among themselves,
the leafy day, the branched night
in harmonious succession –
natural, again, most natural –
as when at length the living God
like living water
let his creatures stand up. Natural.

Penn took a fork from his pocket
as if he meant to swallow meat, at which
the creatures shuddered in their forms, and did
not creep away to weep. Tears,
which are the edge of grief, started like blood,
the animals whining in upstart pain,
abandoned now, to be love's careless victims,
in that compact never to kill. They thought
but little after that of love, as if
love, a watery human element – *in that*
destructive element immerse – were fit
for breaking, the lesser magnitude than care,
or God. Then Fox's tears dropped
shrewdly, determined as a martyr's.

JON SILKIN

A Trip to Millom

*(for Norman Nicholson on his
seventieth birthday)*

In Frizington, Cleator Moor, and Egremont
faith in landscape's undermined; and yet I could
half-believe that, under sunlight, love
had workings there, that what might save us
was alive. I was scouting things that speak
of you: caustic glaring waves to west,
Windscale's stinkhorn towers, Black Combe.

May weather – and, that day, Black Combe
all smiles; Millom, your town, the town
you've given whispers to, a brood of shops
and garages, cheerful under it. There,
in your father's house, and yours, a tray
with glasses and a favourite Malt...

You've always shown me how to recognise.
So it's your making that I know this place,
feel at home in streets that seem
busy about your poetry all day, and stare
through windows on to roofs and frontages
of thirty years' imaginings and look a truth
full in the face: that home's a belonging –
continuity of slate and stone for you; for me,
a kind of luggage dragged around.

MATT SIMPSON

For Norman Nicholson

I see Yvonne and you in nineteen sixty-six
With both of us, both boths standing in Beckermet
Discussing mosses and, I think, liverwort
When a lively wind slammed more quickly down the street
Than anything but the occasional Norton,
Some young lad up, pursuing hell for leather –
And time had come for your eleven hundred
To head off South from that small terraced house we had
And lived in three quick years. The sixties: a decade
Which is meant to mean in general retrospect
Great seismic shifts of taste and values, word for which
Was placed in verse by dry stonewalling Larkin,
As well as all the ready-mix journalists.
It was never my feeling then and is not now.
Yes, fells have fashions and the hemlines rise or fall
But only through Man's pastoral activities:
Their skylines are drawn by sky and rock, not Man,
As Wordsworth saw it; as Wordsworth saw also
That the spirit which is in Man shapes up to them
And what he does truest must stand against the fell;
I see that as a test your work has stood; and shall.

MICHAEL STANDEN

A Dream of Stones

I dreamed a summer's labour,
loss or discovery,
had brought me, on the sand,
to a nest of stones.
What shall I do with these stones
that shine too weakly to be gems,
that might be seeds?

Stones are to build with,
but here there has to be
sand to the sea, bare land and sea.

Why, since these stones
are moist and heavy with sacrifice,
should they not be planted?
There are no trees here.
Maybe there are trees
coiled in the wilderness
of the stone seeds.

I am pocking the soil with my heel.
Here, here, here, here.
Into each footprint, a glimmering pearl.

They will not be counted,
these seeds, these stones, these
possible offerings from impossible language.
They resist being tears.
I tell them to you now as if they were things
too alive to be left unburied
under common years.

                                    ANNE STEVENSON

Windows, Shadows

A single carriage whose quartet of ghosts
dies in faint echoes to both left and right;
    mirrors and windows
where one man's letter moves in darker light
he may not read by, and a third man boasts
    a clutch of shadows.

We rush across the landscape like a fake
legation. Can we speak with the same voice
    despite the windows?
Exclusive as they are they leave a choice
between perfections, though it's a mistake
    to count on shadows.

It's freezing here. Beyond is a whole range,
a gallery of portraits that belong
    only to windows.
Yet something on this side will faintly long
to shadow letters, faces, and exchange
    a life for shadows.

No companion could be more attached.
No brother show a greater sympathy
    than these black windows
making fiction out of fiction, and a body
out of nothing. Some windows may be touched
    only by shadows.

GEORGE SZIRTES

The Bank

Meditating upon gold
we prick the heart on its thorns.

Yellow, yellow, yellow hair
of the spring, the poet cries

admiring the gorse bushes
by the old stone wall. But the maiden's

hair overflows the arms
of the hero. Though you sit down

a thousand years, the echo
of the petals is inaudible

in the sunlight. Explain to me
why we use the same word

for the place we store our money in
and that other place where the gorse blows.

R. S. THOMAS

Second After Trinity

Nine in the congregation. A clergyman
Who's filling in this Sunday: Austrian, Pole,
Some accent I can't place. Why is he here
(Our usual's off, I know: he told us last
Sunday – trivial details lost in church),
But why this foreigner, whose voice is stranger
Even than 1662? But then, there follows
The question, *Why are we here?*, who duly follow
This staid, familiar, dignified, dead rite.
The ritual itself takes over, just;
And unaccompanied (the organ's off)
We sing two hymns we know but don't quite know,
And speak the words, and slowly up the aisle
Follow the other seven who have come,
Knowing they must, with questions of their own.

ANTHONY THWAITE

The Well

We loosen the coping-stone that has sealed for years
    The mid-field well. We slide-off this roof
That has taken root. We cannot tell
    How the single, pale tendril of ivy
Has trailed inside nor where
    In the dark it ends. Past the dark
A small, clear mirror sends
    Our images back to us, the trees
Framing the roundel that we make,
    A circling frieze that answers to the form
Of this tunnel, coiled cool in brick.
    We let down the plumbline we have improvised
Out of twine and a stone, and as it arrives,
    Sounding and sounding past round on round of wall,
Our images liquidly multiply, flow out
    And past all bounds to drown in the dazzle
As a laugh of light runs echoing up from below.

CHARLES TOMLINSON

54

Pay Day

'At the end of the world,' said the crone
'Are blue and red days
Wrapped and waiting in the shade
And yours for the taking.'

I set one foot on the porch,
The boards creaked. The crone
Looked up from her sleeping with a start.
'The chillis are under the cloth,' she said,
'But they ain't been paid for.'

HUGO WILLIAMS

Hemlock

I have drawn up
All that is doubtful in the earth.
Mist gathers in my stem.

When I nod my head late at night
The air fills up with dust
And the books with ignorance.

HUGO WILLIAMS

To Norman Nicholson

As the crow flies we live quite near each other:
But the crow never flies across those mountains,
Those lakes and valleys, rivers and small streams.
Walls crawling up impossible slopes to skies
Blue as an eye or ponderous with rain.

All that we must avoid if we're to reach you:
We go by Workington, to catch the diesel
Edging along a bleak polluted coastline,
Dead foundries, slagheaps, and the yellow flower
Of smoke above Whitehaven; Windscale's dome.

And then there's Ravenglass, and the bird-haunted
Sand-dunes lagooning a derelict sea.
This, Norman, is your country and your home,
And where your verse lives rooted like a tree
To where it grows, feeding its leaves therefrom.

DAVID WRIGHT

The Laureate of the Lakes

Norman reads like a Bard. A Bard homespun and local, a Bard with the eye of a botanist and a gravelled voice witness and consequence of his long illness, but nonetheless a Bard. The side whiskers billow out like two pewter side grips on a prize cup, the declamatory pose continues the prize-speaking theme: Norman was bred for this. To read with him, as I did most memorably in Grasmere Church, is to be abducted to the lost world of that deep and rich chapel and church culture of the ordinary man which he writes about so exactly in *Wednesday Early Closing*. Here is Eloquence reaching out to Expectation: here the Word is sent quivering into the minds and hearts of the Multitude. As Wordsworth counselled the Aeolian harp for the fullest effect of his verse, so might Norman ask for a place of worship and an Occasion; a Time to Shine. Grasmere Church - overspilling on that fund-raising evening - provided him with all of that and the ancient walls happily soaked up the resonating rhythms of this rooted modern poet, the finest Cumbrian born since Wordsworth, the undisputed laureate of the Lakes.

Norman Nicholson's poems were not 'set' books at my Grammar School - even though it is in the same county as Millom, only a few miles north. We stopped at the Romantics. Wordsworth was thoroughly done, though, and one of the many consequences of that was a capacity to enter into Norman's world through the same mountain passes of Wordsworth over which he himself has been found to trudge.

All regional writers have a powerful view of that Indisputably Great Author who has gone before them in what is still, to a large extent, much the same circumscribed place. Place, in another sense like Plot: the nature and mystery of which has, it seems, already been unravelled, revealed and manifested. Wordsworth appears to own not only the Cumbrian landscape, and in so many particulars of local denomination - he seems to own the response we have to it. Not entirely surprising in that our present response was largely received through the education of his insights. For those of us born there, though, there is the underlying resentment - which sometimes shows itself as bewilderment. Are any feelings and reactions we have before what we were born into anything more than an imitation? Or are they necessarily and at best, the variation on a theme set in lines of poetry which scatter over the history of literature like megaliths?

Norman seems to have seen Wordsworth, in one aspect, as a devil to be exorcised, not from himself but from what he saw. He described this to me as we were forging down Coniston on that superbly refurbished Gondola. He spoke of it in detail and with care, attempting strictly to distinguish but in the end it was much as if he were crudely and simply dividing up the territory. Almost, indeed, in a way, as if he were saying – let Wordsworth take the High Ground, I'll take the Low Ground.

For all his adult life that has been literally true. Living in a district most outstanding for the variety and prospects offered by its fells, Norman's view of it has always been from the valleys. It seems to me, though, that he has not spent and certainly not wasted much time looking up: he has kept his eyes firmly in front of his feet and discovered an evident relish for botany, geology and the rumps and remains from previous cultures – especially the Norse and most specifically for our dialect's verbal inheritance from that; the most explosive invasion of Cumbria Norse words glint in his verse like crystalline intrusions.

The illness which has been such a shaper of his life and, possibly, his art, has resulted in what appears to me to be a curious stance, pose almost, vis-à-vis Millom and the country around it. The bedrock is sternly local in all that profusion of lower middle class northern industrial life which, from the comparatively safe spy-hole of his father's shop, streamed past him already a little pre-selected. In the self-protective and self-projecting madhouse of the English class system, the Nicholsons were not Nobody: not by any means. Their foothold in independence, aspiration and a sort of gentility gave him a vivid view of life which – so old fashioned is a decaying industrial town and so cut off has the north west always been – I could still find in my own childhood sixty years on. It is a world into which he moves easily from Dickens: in character and condition there are no walls between the mid-Victorian fiction and the early twentieth century reality. Goitres, malnutrition, 'characters', brave and perky claims to life, nonconformists. This is where I think Norman most closely touches on Cumbria and in his autobiography, as in those poems which deal with people or industrial life, he achieves the condition of chronicler as well as poet.

Millom, which could have been his millstone, became his base camp. For those of us brought up in quiet low northern towns – glittering with child life but subject to desertion by adults as the social landscape thins down to work, booze and sport – Norman's accomplishment is not a small one. He engaged the great art in a place where few if any at all regarded it as anything but a blank joke. He quarried around and about the deserted slag heaps of a cruelly transient industry, often averting his eyes, looking more at the plants than the old workings; but never turning away his mind. It has always been bare pickings on the coast of Cumbria, yet he gathered enough and more for a lifetime of sustaining verse, combining the beaches and the valleys, living light. If I regret what could – fruitfully, I think – have been his greater engagement with the people of that place, then that is little more than an expression of my greed to see an even larger exhibition of his talent. There was a sense in which he had to turn from the people of Millom: and yet he will always be the Millom poet. He is read by Cumbrian students today and no mistake.

The casting of himself as the observer, the onlooker often results in a laconic, even peremptory way with people. This, though, is a hard and true way of caring. Nothing is wasted on sentimentality or admitted dreaming. From Millom, Norman inherited no nonsense, no 'show', no fat.

Although his knowledge of the place is deep, there is, when you meet him, something so reserved about his expression of that affinity, something so careful and almost pedantic about it that you sense how deeply he wants to or has to keep it at a distance. In order to survive at all when he came back from the South, only partly on the mend from his time in the sanatorium with T.B., he had to turn his back on the sooty, smoky town and make for the fresh air. His interrupted studies and desire to learn found an object in the flowers and birds of the area: his ambition conspired to lead him to authorship. All of this was a cutting off from that humble jumble of riches in his town past.

For there is another sense in which Norman is not a 'local' poet nor has he ever, I think, greatly wanted to be. The fact that he was pinned down in cut-off declining Millom seems to have spurred him on to prove and assert that he could reach out to the centre in his work. The metropolitan poets who emerged in the thirties meant more to him as a developing poet, I would guess, than all the greatness of Wordsworth, all the lure of the pastoral-parochial. The result is a seeming aloofness, possibly a saving distinction from too much cleaving to a place which had given him life but threatened to destroy his ability to support it.

Which is why Norman seems to me most himself when he is on some podium or other. In the formality of his kitchen you drink tea out of fragile china cups. In a general conversation you soon come up against the rich monologues and sudden full-stops of one who lived and came through - for much of the time - alone. Whenever I saw him with Yvonne he was very happy, but outside that intimacy which is forbidden to all but a very few - and in Norman's case I suspect even fewer than most - I feel I know him best when he gets to his feet as he did on many an early platform when he was a boy. Then he seems easy and at rest with his Cumbrian audiences - not one of them, though truly from them, keeping that cosseted distance which helped him to live, someone who has set himself apart, in thought, word and deed and who comes back from the long journey inside himself to deliver the messages learnt in the place he could never leave.

MELVYN BRAGG

A Lifetime's Effort

for Norman at 70

Norman Nicholson began to write poems almost fifty years ago, in 1937; oddly enough, for a poet who has spent all his life in his birthplace of Millom in Cumbria, his first poem to be published, 'Song for 7 p.m.', appeared in America, in *Poetry (Chicago)* in March, 1938. Since then his long career as England's most deeply-rooted regional poet has been both distinguished and lonely, and effectively divided into two parts by the eighteen-year gap which yawns, like the abandoned mine-workings of Millom, between his third collection *The Pot Geranium* (1954) and its successor *A Local Habitation* (1972). Before that wide lacuna, partly accounted for by a seven-year poetic silence, Nicholson could be seen as a Christian poet who, first, simply happened to live in a small industrial town in Cumbria, but who later, in broadcasts like 'On Being a Provincial', sprang to the defence of its virtues against suspected metropolitan prejudice. By the 1970s attitudes had changed, regional magazines and presses were defying the whip of literary London, and Nicholson was praised by a new generation of poets and critics as a writer of solid, consistent local integrity who had no need to justify his kind of subject matter. But in both periods, whatever their fashions, the merits of Nicholson's work brought their rewards: the Heinemann Prize, and a fellowship of the Royal Society of Literature, in 1945, Poetry Book Society Choices, the Queen's Medal for Poetry, Arts Council grants, honorary degrees culminating in a Litt.D. from Liverpool University, and, most recently, the O.B.E. The epigraph to his most recent volume, *Sea to the West* (1981), though appropriate in coming from his earliest influence, W. H. Auden, is in no way necessary: it has been clear for many years that Nicholson's 'local valley cheese' is 'prized elsewhere'.

Nicholson's poetic technique in *Sea to the West* is as skilful as ever: over nearly five decades he has moved with great adroitness from sonnet and lyrical stanza to the most flexible blank verse and the strictest syllabic metre, and here, in poems like 'Weeds' and 'Do You Remember Adlestrop?', he displays an impressive blend of conversational ease and musical intricacy. In much of its material and atmosphere, however, the volume hints at finality. Reading it for the first time, and responding to the almost visionary intensity of its many images

61

of light, I was reminded of Rosamond Lehmann's recent, retrospective novel *A Sea-Grape Tree*, whose last sentence reads: 'Dissolved in light, the hut, the sea-grape tree have disappeared.' The title-poem recalls the dazzling sunsets of youth and the comforting darkness 'like an eiderdown' that followed them; but the prospect of death, at 'Five times, perhaps, fifteen', leaves Nicholson asking:

> Let my eyes at the last be blinded
> Not by the dark
> But by dazzle.

Less mystical attitudes to 'last things' are conveyed in 'At the Musical Festival', which (as in such earlier poems as 'Five Minutes', 'Rising Five' and 'Old Man at a Cricket Match') takes a local phrase — 'giving it Wigan' — in order to stress the necessity for courage in the face of the ultimate 'class and adjudication'; and also in the less contrived and far finer poem 'The New Cemetery', which compares the release of railway horses from their weekday work to the poet's final 'unblinkered' and joyous freedom from his 'life-time's/Load of parcels'.

The volume, like its four Faber predecessors, has many felicitous phrases which arouse one's professional admiration and envy: pebbles on the shore 'smooth as butterbeans' (in 'Shingle'); boys in the 1920s, 'Their big toes squirting through their boots' (in 'Comprehending it Not', which also ends with images of light and darkness); the sight of the signature of Nicholson's old headmaster in 'The Register': 'A recognized unrecognition faded bluely on the page'; 'a cataract of known appearances' in the splendidly dense virtuoso piece 'Landing on Staffa', whose unaccustomed glimpse of Nicholson as a tourist gives place, at the end, to his more usual determination to describe the hitherto undescribed in his home town.

Millom, however, is not the place it was. In 'Midsummer Fires on the Sognefjord', whose response to things Norwegian recalls Nicholson's enthusiastic linking of Norway and Cumberland in 'For the Grieg Centenary' (*Five Rivers*), an unusually limpid line serves well to characterise the sense of an ending which this collection gives: 'The track through the orchard slowly fills with midnight'. The many poems of inanimate nature, reminiscent of those in *Rock Face* (1948), which occupy a third of the book, convey not only nature's energy (as in 'Plankton') but the impermanence of many of her forms — as in 'Dunes', 'Tide Out', 'Shingle' and 'Beck', in which even 'Ingleborough and Helvellyn/Waste daily away'.

So too must Scafell Pike, though in the opening poem Nicholson chooses to present the mountain in relation to the human time-scale, as surviving the depopulated Millom of the future from which the reader is somewhat illogically instructed to observe it.

The contrast, and sometimes the parallelism, of the human and the natural worlds have habitually served Nicholson as images of time and eternity; the finest example in Nicholson's work of this kind of poem is his sequence 'The Seven Rocks', first published in Cyril Connolly's *Horizon* in 1948. A chilling specimen of his awareness of the non-human scale in this volume is 'Fjord', but his imaginative empathy and sheer descriptive gifts are equally apparent in the many other poems of water, earth and rock in *Sea to the West*. But the real emotional power of the volume — a bleak power — is embodied in the final group of a dozen or so poems, in which Nicholson insistently harks back to the industrial past of his home town, and to his own childhood, and contrasts them implicitly or explicitly with the present. At the end of 'Midsummer Fires on the Sognefjord' Nicholson connects Norway in summer with Millom on Guy Fawkes' Night, seeing in the bonfire of 'heaped sleepers and old bicycle tyres . . . on a Cumbrian slagbank' a 'Faint reek of ancestral fires'. The fires are a whisper of Norse heritage; but, more bitterly, they are also the relics of Millom's past as a thriving steel-making town, where 'midnight sunsets' were 'ladled across a cloudy sky'.

The poem in which that line occurs, 'On the Dismantling of Millom Ironworks', takes decline one stage further than 'On the Closing of Millom Ironworks', written in 1968 and printed in *A Local Habitation*. Packed, muscular, burning with a subdued anger of remembered factual detail, the poem makes painfully clear the traumatic effect on Nicholson of the addition of insult to injury, the destruction of a hundred years of communal life:

> They cut up the carcass of the old ironworks
> Like a fat beast in a slaughterhouse: they shovelled my childhood
> On to a rubbish heap . . . . .

Nicholson's laughter at Wordsworth, in 'To the River Duddon' (*Five Rivers*), boomerangs back at him; now, indeed, the Duddon is truly becoming 'Remote from every taint of sordid industry'. (I recall vividly my own shock and bewilderment, revisiting Millom in the late 1970s, and seeing an enormous blank across the sky where once the great battleship of the ironworks had poured out its smoke.) A similar bitter regret runs through 'The Bloody Cranesbill', and makes understandable Nicholson's desperate need to celebrate the survival of the flower which 'in a lagoon of despoliation . . . /Still grows today'. Like Halley's Comet, its celestial analogue in the poem of 1975 printed at the end of the volume, the flower provides a frail link with the past of vanished ancestors 'As the town my mind still lives in crumbles dustily round me' ('The Register'). Such involvement with his locality and its fortunes has always been a primary aspect of Nicholson's poetry: in this volume, 'Glen Orchy', with its final desolate picture of 'smokeless furnace chimneys' and 'five hundred men/At one stroke out of work', comes full circle back to an unpublished poem of 1937, 'By the Sea', which reacted, less concisely but with great force, to the industrial depression of the 1930s.

Sea to the West is a powerful and distinctive collection. At seventy, though, a poet as good as Norman Nicholson deserves to be represented in print by more than his latest volume, its predecessor of twelve years ago, and a slim *Selected Poems* more than half of whose contents dates from 1965 and is still easily obtained elsewhere. I make no complaint about the poems it includes; they would win many new readers for Nicholson's poetry. But as one who first read Nicholson as a teenager in the 1950s, I am sorry at the amount it excludes; it is as if, to use Proust's vibrant image at the end of *Time Regained*, Nicholson were not standing high on the tall stilts of his whole poetic life but had chosen to draw up much of his past behind him like a rope ladder. The true perspective of his long career requires a beginning and a middle, as well as an end (though one hopes that *Sea to the West* is not that). His description of his work, in 'Cornthwaite', as 'my peck of poems, not much of a crop', is absurdly modest; but it is unfortunately true to say that, of the nearly 200 poems he has published in volumes, little more than a third are currently available outside libraries; not to speak of the more than two dozen poems, including the lively and characteristic 'On Suspected Dry Rot in the Roof of a Parish Church', left to fade bluely between the covers of scattered magazines. What is needed now — the best tribute to Nicholson, and the best *Festschrift* for his readers old and new — is a full-scale *Collected Poems*, a bushel which would display within one set of covers the full range and vigour of his unique achievement, as a poet who has combined in memorable speech the regional and the universal, the world perceived and the world created.

PHILIP GARDNER

Books by Norman Nicholson

(Place of publication, London, unless otherwise stated)
POETRY

An Anthology of Religious Verse.   Penguin.   1942

Selected Poems: John Hall, Keith Douglas and Norman Nicholson.   Bale and Staples.   1943

Five Rivers.   Faber.   1944

Rock Face.   Faber.   1948

The Pot Geranium.   Faber.   1954

Selected Poems.   Faber.   1966

No Star on the Way Back.   Manchester, Manchester Institute of Contemporary Arts.   1967

A Local Habitation.   Faber.   1972

Stitch and Stone.   Sunderland, Ceolfrith Press.   1975

The Shadow of Black Combe.   Ashington, Mid-Northumberland Arts Group.   1978

Sea to the West.   Faber.   1981

Selected Poems 1940-1982.   Faber.   1982

The Candy-Floss Tree: Norman Nicholson, Gerda Mayer and Frank Flynn.   Oxford, O.U.P.   1984

PLAYS

The Old Man of the Mountains.   Faber.   1946

Prophesy to the Wind.   Faber.   1950

A Match for the Devil.   Faber.   1955

Birth by Drowning.   Faber.   1960

NOVELS

The Fire of the Lord.   Nicholson and Watson.   1944

The Green Shore.   Nicholson and Watson.   1947

LITERARY CRITICISM AND BIOGRAPHY

Man and Literature.   S.C.M. Press.   1943

Wordsworth: an Introduction and Selection.   Phoenix House.   1949

H. G. Wells.   Barker.   1950

William Cowper.   Lehmann.   1951

William Cowper.   Longmans, Green/British Council.   1960

A Choice of Cowper's Verse.   Faber.   1975

LOCAL

Cumberland and Westmorland.   Hale.   1949

The Lakers.   Hale.   1955

Provincial Pleasures.   Hale.   1959

Portrait of the Lakes.   Hale.   1963

Greater Lakeland.   Hale.   1969

The Lakes.   Hale.   1977

The Lake District: an anthology.   Hale.   1977
                                  Penguin.   1978

AUTOBIOGRAPHY

Wednesday Early Closing.   Faber.   1975

MISCELLANEOUS

Enjoying it All.   Waltham Forest Books.   1964

Bibliography compiled by
GEORGE BOTT